An Hour From Never

Talia Wright

Presentation by *BookLeaf Publishing*

Web: www.bookleafpub.com

E-mail: info@bookleafpub.com

ISBN: 978-93-5744-469-9

First edition 2022

DEDICATION

To my wonderful parents who have always supported and encouraged me. Thank you for telling me to sit down and write. You are amazing and I love you both.

ACKNOWLEDGEMENT

I would like to acknowledge that this book has been carried on my belief that I can use the English language in whichever way I please.

I let the moment seize me and for that, I do not apologise. I am proud of what I have accomplished in this novel. No matter how disjointed, disorganised and altogether too much like me, this book is.

I hope you find some part of these poems that resonates with you.

PREFACE

I chose to enter this competition to get into a habit of writing every day. That did not happen. I wrote every couple of days when I wasn't too tired or busy or when I had an idea or a few and I was ready to sit down and write. Maybe that wasn't the spirit of the game, maybe that wasn't the task I was given but that's how it went.
I have enjoyed writing these. Seeing how my mood affected what I wrote on any given day. How the people I had spoken to, the things I'd watched and the books I'd read had changed how I saw the world.
If this challenge has taught me anything, it's that I am still very good at working under pressure and to a time frame.

I bid you adieu, until next time.
- Talia Wright

I Wish for the Genius

In childhood we are taught to shield ourselves.
We mask, we control, we order.
We are tasked with the impossible.
Not only to grow up, but to conform.
School teaches us that we are imperfect.
That others' judgements matter more than our
own,
That our worth is determined by that of our
peers.
We are graded, given strict perimeters
Our individuality,
Our creativity,
Is molded,
Sliced,
Put into a box so small,
So far out of reach,
We are left with numbers.
Our parents remember when we were young,
When we were creative and inspired.
When the genius spoke directly to us, worked
through us.
As we grow, we forget.

We forget our initial calling to that 'thing' we
loved.
We lose the sense of self that made us
individuals
And instead, we are left with what we were
made for,
Production lines.
I wish I could say the future is changing.
I wish I could say that my young cousins will be
nurtured
Their creativity embraced.
If only we didn't have to work so hard to
recapture that 'childish' curiosity.
I miss those stories the adults called silly.
I miss the free spirit that was me.

At home in the trees

Pines are my favourite.
Tall, sturdy,
Mostly symmetrical.
They are useful and beautiful,
Padding the ground with their debris.
They make me think of mountains, covered in
green,
Yet equally of the beach, family and sunshine.
Funny how an image so different can be created
by one object.
Parrot trees remind me of home. The constant
squawking at all hours,
The massive noticeable growth after heavy rain.
The eerie deathlike quality they get in winter.
The smell of chlorine from the pool below.
While pine trees remind me of calm and fun,
Parrot trees will always mean home to me.

Goodbye, Dear One

I didn't wear perfume.
I wore an outfit I won't wear again.
I cried.
We've been expecting it for a while now,
The day we'd have to say goodbye.
But only days ago
We thought that you were fine.
But we know that you were in pain,
And that it was long past time.
But we loved every second we had you,
Our little woolly friend.
We'll miss you every day.
And never forget our dear poodle,
If only you could have stayed.

It's All in The Age

The glittery feeling.
A warm sensation,
One that starts just beside each eye and ripples
throughout your body,
Cooling only at your fingertips, as they grip the
glass.
Booze.
Our one constant.
The thing many of us enjoy, others rely on,
And most of us abuse mercilessly,
Swearing on those terrible mornings
'we'll never drink again'
Only to do it the following week.
It's a terrifically terrible trial.
And yet…

Exhaustion

I hold my breath and fall.
Into the spiral of apathy.
The all-consuming deprivation
Of care, resilience, and hope.
Some days are easier,
Others I want to curl up
Avoid the world
Screaming "just one more hour",
One more minute.
I'm tired,
So, so tired.

Family

I spend a lot of my time with family,
Around them, thinking about them.
The unconditional love.
It keeps me going, grounded.
They taught me that love,
Although sometimes distant and unsaid,
Is always there.
In the hugs when we unite,
In the words through the phone,
In the happy birthday voice messages.
In the birthday cards signed with love.
My home is my family,
My family my home.

An Imposter

I call myself a reader.
A consumer of fiction.
Yet I spend my time doing anything else.
So much of my life has been,
Identifying myself as one thing.
An intelligent being,
A hoarder of worlds.
A creator of them,
occasionally.
I fall into the stories,
I change my persona to match that of the lead.
I adapt.
I change.
I become.
Until I can no longer tell where I,
The original,
Fit in.
I am the product of my imagination.
And I wouldn't have it any other way.

The City

It's never truly dark in the city.
The closer you get, the brighter the world glows.
It's funny how decay can do that.
Light up the world.
It will kill us, but at least it helps,
Now.
The country has light too.
But it's the unobtrusive light,
The light of a thousand stars
Far off galaxies burning so brightly
They light our way.
As your eyes adjust.
Remember,
You too are lighting someone else's way.
In another world, in another time.

Kaleidoscope

Objectively speaking,
I'm a bit of a nutcase.
I imagine myself,
My true self from when I was young,
As a blank canvas.
Every person, character.
Place and story
Have added their own colours.
I am a product of the things I admire.
The things I notice.
The things I find interesting, intriguing.
Everyday, every adventure,
The canvas gets a little more,
Colourful.
A little more,
Curious,
A little more,
Complex.
All the characteristics that make humans
bedazzle.
Continue to brighten your canvas,
Mix the colours
And watch the world flourish,
For it has you,

And me,
And we are spectacularly,
Haphazardly whimsical.

Welcome

I don't write poetry.
You've probably guessed that by now.
So, I thought I should confirm.
I've spent a lot of my life convinced I was going
to be a writer.
A creator of fiction.
Apparently, I decided it when I was very young.
I told my parents that's what I wanted to be,
I don't even remember doing that.
I tell everyone I meet that I'm a writer.
I like the way it makes me feel,
That I know, in some small way, it's already the
truth.
I love authors.
I have always been able to disappear into a
book.
Yes, it's a form of escapism but the worlds are a
part of me now.
I continue to treasure the thought that I might
one day publish.
But for now, please enjoy this book of poems.

Why fear an outcome that hasn't happened yet?

I finished a book today.
I've been putting it off for a while.
Expecting heart-break,
Weeping,
Massive book hangover.
But I did it,
I survived.
It was startlingly tragic,
Beautifully written,
But not all together miserable as I had feared.
I should have finished it long ago,
But I was so afraid of the outcome, I didn't.
I have wasted two months,
I could have read so much more,
Done so much more.
What a lesson to be learnt in a book.

500 Words or Less

I wrote a story once.
About the limitations of a word limit.
The need that is placed on young people,
To confine their creativity into a box,
A set amount of words.
Where description and emotion is sacrificed
For the progression of a plot.
Unique thought is slaughtered by the quick
cliches,
That are easiest to explain
The ordinary and familiar replace
That which allows a story to flourish.
I wrote a story,
Over the word limit,
Exceeding the confines.
It was praised for its creativity,
Of course it was,
It is impossible to write a decent story,
In 500 words or less.

Melancholy on my drive

I slowed down to look at a tree today.
I thought it was rather novel for me.
I'm a bit of a rally driver when I'm by myself.
It was dusk,
On a road I drive almost daily.
A tree I've seen a million times,
It was that time of night when the lights are all
on but the sun is just slightly still visible on the
horizon.
When you're never quite sure whether you need
your headlights on or not.
Looking to the other drivers to make the
decision for you.
The tree, a massive one in the middle of a
round-a-bout.
Far too big for its little home,
Pressing itself against the lights meant to
illuminate the road beneath.
The entirety of its foliage a deep, rich emerald
green,
Everywhere but where the warm glow of the
light touched it.

There it was a yellowish-brown.
The contrast was startling,
But that time of night has always been my
favourite,
The trees moody and vibrant.
And so, I slowed down to marvel for a moment,
Then continued with my day.

Procrastination- And to the Devil take Ye

I've always been good at last minute.
Procrastinating,
Wasting time,
Finding everything else to be doing before doing
the one thing I was meant to.
In assessment time at school,
The windows of the house would be clean,
The floors swept and mopped,
My sheets clean, and my clothes folded.
I would even rearrange the furniture in my room,
Claiming when asked, "the change will help me
think better".
It never did but I liked the excuse.
So here I am,
Once again having left everything to the last
minute.
I did have an excuse this time.
I'll tell you all about it if you ask.

Embrace ALL

I've never considered myself a particularly
pretty individual.
As I get older, I've started to like me more and
more.
I look at photos of myself when I was little,
That awkward stage between puberty and adult,
The purgatory where nothing is quite working
together.
As I aged, I got taller,
My body curved,
My face elongated.
I started to gain more confidence.
I like me a lot more now,
Not that I ever didn't like myself,
I just recognise my thoughts better now.
But you know what really saved me.
My hair.
I've always loved it.
I can't leave the house without being
complimented at least once.
I love it more and more every day.
I embrace the 'you look like that princess, yeah
the Scottish one!'
It makes me feel good.

When my cousin runs over with any and all
red-headed dolls proclaiming
"look, it's you!" – she brightens my day.
So yes, I might sometimes have problems with
other parts of me,
The small knit-picking we all do while staring at
individual parts,
Opposed to marvelling at how all those parts
work simultaneously
To make up the wonderful whole.
I will always love my fiery hair,
And my matching personality.

Incomparable Perhaps

Ever wanted to be unique?
Maybe not consciously,
But I'm sure we all do.
I most certainly try sometimes but mostly it
happens naturally.
I read – check one
I write – check two
I review books,
Collect vinyls,
Shop in boutiques
Watch plays instead of going out and
Research obscure historical events
Check, check, check, check.
As I spend more time in the world.
Surrounded by people a little more like me,
I realise,
I'm not actually that unique.
And I'm ok with that.
I think we should be.
Embrace those who like what we like,
Don't belittle those who don't,

And just do whatever the fuck you want,
Because who's watching anyway?

Faults can be Somewhat a Virtue

We're almost at the end,
How exciting.
Now I do realise that I have failed this
challenge,
Rather spectacularly I might add.
I haven't written every day,
I've barely written every three days,
But we've made it.
And I'm glad.
I've made very little effort to refine these,
My raw thoughts are what you've got.
My 'inspiration of the moment' –
Lacking forethought,
Or in fact, hindsight as I have not read them
back.
Yet we've made it, and I'm proud.
So please enjoy my last-ditch effort as we dash
toward the finish.
Please proceed.

Be Like the Time

There are many things I resonate with.
Most of these do happen to be pop culture,
A somewhat unfortunate realisation
Considering the price of my education,
But none the less,
It is true.
I live life with quotes from movies,
Emotions I have carried off the page,
Songs I've sung at the top of my lungs playing,
On repeat it my head.
Despite the excessive amount of classics I read,
Regardless of my obsession with history,
And antiquity,
All those things that seem otherworldly,
Proper,
Beautiful.
Instead of those things,
I voluntarily choose to beguile the time and the
people around me,
with utter nonsense.
I could feel remorse.
For deceiving the people around, me,
Into calling thinking me more than extraordinary
than I am,
But where is the fun in that?

der Bruder

I am many things.
I am a granddaughter, daughter, cousin and
friend.
But for all my life,
Since the second I first breathed air,
I've been a little sister.
Now you might say I've been many of the other
things my whole life as well,
But I consider the last the most important.
My older brother is always there for me.
A friend,
Someone to spend time with when I was little,
To protect and teach me as I got older.
He's the reason I am who I am today.
Despite our fighting,
Our numerous disagreements,
I will always be proud to call him my brother.

By Degree

The funny thing about burns is they don't really
hurt the moment you get them.
There's an instant,
A moment where your only thought is to move
away from the heat.
The reflex of withdrawing,
Sheltering your body from the external.
Only to have searing pain follow the momentary
release.
A throbbing that doesn't go away without cold,
running water.
Weeks go by with the mark,
If you're lucky it might go way,
Or you'll be left with a little bit forever,
A reminder, barely distinct enough to find.
But you know it's there,
And you live with it.

Gap Year Failed

I wouldn't consider myself gifted.
Most people talk about gifted kid burnout.
But what about just plain old burnout?
I tried hard in school,
I got the best grades I could on the lack of
revision I did.
Leaving assignments until the last minute,
Revision even later than that.
But when I finished school,
After the enormous finals cramming,
I basically collapsed.
I was exhausted.
It took me months to pick up a book,
A year later,
A year of intense work schedules at a shitty job,
I'm still exhausted,
Not at all prepared to face the day,
Or the new year at university.